3rd Edition
Start Quilting

with Alex Anderson

Everything First-Time Quilters Need to Succeed

•

8 Quick Projects—Most in 4 Sizes

C&T PUBLISHING

Publisher: Amy Marson

Creative Director: Gailen Runge

Editor: Liz Aneloski

Technical Editor: Sandy Peterson

Copyeditor/Proofreader: Wordfirm Inc.

Cover/Book Designer: Kristy K. Zacharias

Production Coordinator: Kirstie L. Pettersen

Photography by Christina Carty-Francis and Diane Pedersen of C&T Publishing, Inc., unless otherwise noted.

Published by C&T Publishing, Inc., P.O. Box 1456, Lafayette, CA 94549

Library of Congress Cataloging-in-Publication Data
Anderson, Alex.
  Start quilting with Alex Anderson : everything first-time quilters need to succeed : 8 quick projects-most in 4 sizes. -- 3rd ed.
     p. cm.
  ISBN 978-1-57120-812-5 (paper trade)
  1. Patchwork--Patterns. 2. Quilting--Patterns. 3. Patchwork quilts. I. Title.

TT835.A5234 2009
746.46'041--dc22

                          2009004907

    Printed in China

10 9 8 7 6 5 4 3

Dedication

To Pam Vieira-McGinnis, queen celebrity stunt sewer. Thank you for your keen eye and swift hands—this book would not have been possible without you.

Acknowledgments

Thank you to Todd and Tony Hensley for your continued support; Liz Aneloski for keeping me on track and for being so generous with your time; Mark Aneloski for being my project carrier pigeon; Olfa, Omnigrid, P&B Textiles, Moda Fabrics, Maywood Studio, Hoffman Fabrics, and Superior Threads for providing excellent products; Erica for your eagle eye; Cindy Carvalho and my friends at Alden Lane Nursery for your help and support; John Vitale for your creative eye; John who puts up with my crazy lifestyle; and last but not least, my cousin Lauren Marlotte for her killer poppy seed cake.

Contents

Introduction

A quilt is like a sandwich. It has three layers:

The quilt top is usually made of many 100% cotton fabrics that are cut in various sizes and then sewn together, either by hand or by machine. This is called piecing.

The middle layer, called the batting, is usually either polyester or cotton.

The backing is another piece of 100% cotton fabric. Cotton fabric is usually 42″ wide; so, if your quilt top exceeds 42″ in width, you will need to sew pieces of fabric together (piece) to create a wide enough piece of fabric for the backing.

All three layers are then stitched together, either by hand or by machine, uniting all three components (pieced top, batting, backing) as one. This is called quilting.

I can remember the first quilt I ever made. My grandma started a Grandmother's Flower Garden quilt in the 1930s and was pleased as punch when I expressed a desire to finish it. What she didn't know was that I was one month and one unit short of graduating from college, and I had contracted the project to fulfill that requirement. I had not only a fantasy of graduating with a bachelor's degree in art, but also dreams of snuggling under my hand-pieced and hand-quilted queen-size quilt on
a cold winter night. Needless to say, I graduated, but with a quilt the size of a bath mat. Although I had originally planned to be a weaver, visions of quilts danced in my head. As they say, "The rest is history." I'm a quilter for life.

I love quilts. During the past three decades, I have been fortunate enough to be a participant in the renaissance and evolution of quiltmaking into a sophisticated art form that offers many different avenues to explore. At

The Quilt Show (www.thequiltshow.com), Ricky Tims and I present expert quilters who share their latest techniques or approaches to quiltmaking. This craft keeps getting more innovative, and there is always a new method on the horizon. I can remember when the quilting world was introduced to rotary cutters, and now we can generate quilts on computers, scan images to print our own fabric, and connect with other quilters worldwide!

Whether this time-honored craft has reached its peak is often discussed. Are there any new quilters out there? The answer is yes, and it is you! I am often asked where a person interested in quilting should begin. So I decided to write this book to get the beginning quilter started with the basics. You must remember that there are many different approaches to quiltmaking, and one is not better than the others, just different.

What this book provides is an introduction to the world of rotary-cut quiltmaking (as opposed to the templates that my grandma used), with eight simple wall quilts you can complete using seven basic 6″ × 6″ finished quilt blocks. Fabric requirements are based on standard 42″-wide fabric.

The term *finished* means that this is the size after the piece has been sewn into the quilt. This size no longer includes the seam allowances. Thus, a 6½″ × 6½″ block becomes 6″ × 6″ finished block once it has been sewn into the quilt.

I recommend that you start with a small project as your first quilt. You will be able to finish it and feel successful. I find that when first-time quilters start with a large project, the whole process becomes overwhelming, and they either give up in frustration or lose the enjoyment of the process. Besides, if you start small, you can begin another quilt sooner.

I will teach you how to make the following seven quilt blocks.

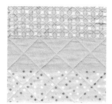

Rail Fence

Nine-Patch Variation

Log Cabin Variation

Friendship Star

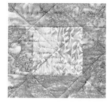

Square Dance

Flying Geese

Nine-Patch

These seven blocks consist of three of the most basic shapes quilters work with all the time: squares, rectangles, and triangles.

If you find that you really enjoy making one of these patterns, you can make more blocks to complete a larger quilt any size you want (see chart below). The width of the borders is just a suggestion; trust your eye to determine the border width that works for your quilt. See Appendix A (pages 44–47) for yardage requirements and cutting instructions for twin, double/queen, and king comforter-style quilts to augment the projects in this book.

My hope for you is that through making these projects, you will become familiar with the basics of quiltmaking and develop into a quilt lover, as I have. Good luck, and don't blame me if your family never sees the whites of your eyes again—they will get used to it.

	STANDARD MATTRESS SIZE	COMFORTER* (6˝ blocks)		COVERLET**(6˝ blocks)		BEDSPREAD*** (6˝ blocks)	
Three-Year Crib	23˝ × 46˝	32˝ × 56˝	4 × 8 blocks, 1˝ inner border, 3˝ outer border	N/A	N/A	N/A	N/A
Six-Year Crib	27˝ × 52˝	40˝ × 64˝	5 × 9 blocks, 1˝ inner border, 4˝ outer border	N/A	N/A	N/A	N/A
Twin	39˝ × 75˝	66˝ × 90˝	9 × 13 blocks, 1˝ inner border, 5˝ outer border	72˝ × 102˝	10 × 15 blocks, 1˝ inner border, 5˝ outer border	78˝ × 108˝	11 × 16 blocks, 1˝ inner border, 5˝ outer border
Full	54˝ × 75˝	78˝ × 90˝	11 × 13 blocks, 1˝ inner border, 5˝ outer border	84˝ × 102˝	12 × 15 blocks, 1˝ inner border, 5˝ outer border	96˝ × 108˝	14 × 16 blocks, 1˝ inner border, 5˝ outer border
Queen	60˝ × 80˝	88˝ × 94˝	12 × 13 blocks, 2˝ inner border, 6˝ outer border	94˝ × 106˝	13 × 15 blocks, 2˝ inner border, 6˝ outer border	100˝ × 112˝	14 × 16 blocks, 2˝ inner border, 6˝ outer border
King	78˝ × 80˝	106˝ × 94˝	15 × 13 blocks, 2˝ inner border, 6˝ outer border	112˝ × 106˝	16 × 15 blocks, 2˝ inner border, 6˝ outer border	118˝ × 112˝	17 × 16 blocks, 2˝ inner border, 6˝ outer border

All measurements reflect finished sizes.
*Comforters cover the mattress but not the box spring; no pillow tuck.
**Coverlets cover the mattress and box spring and have a pillow tuck.
***Bedspreads cover the bed almost to the floor and have a pillow tuck.

tools

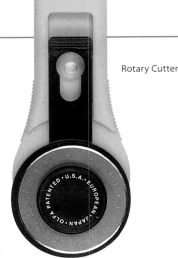

Rotary Cutter

Tools Checklist

See pages 6–7, 18, and 20 for more information.

- Rotary cutter
- Rotary mat
- Rotary ruler
- Scissors
- Pins
- Thread for hand and machine piecing and quilting
- Seam ripper
- Iron
- Sewing machine
- Fabric
- Marking tools for quilting
- Batting
- Masking tape (¼˝ and 1˝ widths)
- Hoop or frame for hand quilting
- Thimble for hand sewing and hand quilting
- Needles for hand and machine sewing and quilting
- Walking foot for machine quilting
- Safety pins for machine quilting

Quilters love gadgets, and every year more tools are introduced to the quilt-making world. Your first visit to a quilt shop or the quilting section of a fabric store can be overwhelming. Many decisions need to be made when purchasing the necessary tools to get started quilting. The following shopping list provides the must-haves for anyone getting started. Many of the products come in different sizes. Please obtain the sizes recommended here. Later, you may want to add companion supplies, but the following are the best sizes to start with. Although the initial investment will seem costly, these tools will serve you for years if taken care of properly. (See pages 16, 18, and 20 for quilting supplies.)

ROTARY CUTTER

This rolling razor blade mounted on a plastic handle is extremely dangerous and should be kept away from young children. I recommend the medium-size (45 mm) cutter.

ROTARY MAT

This self-healing plastic mat must be used in conjunction with the rotary cutter. I recommend either the medium or large mat. The medium one is great for starting out or for taking to a quilting class. The larger one is more versatile. Eventually you will want both sizes. Keep the mat out of direct sunlight and never leave it in a hot car, as the heat will cause the mat to warp and become unusable.

ROTARY RULER

This tool was made especially for use with the rotary cutter and mat. It has ⅛˝ increments marked in both directions and is thick enough not to be cut by the rotary cutter. You will eventually have many rulers; to start with, I recommend a 6˝ × 12˝ rotary ruler. Remove the plastic wrap before using.

Rotary Mat

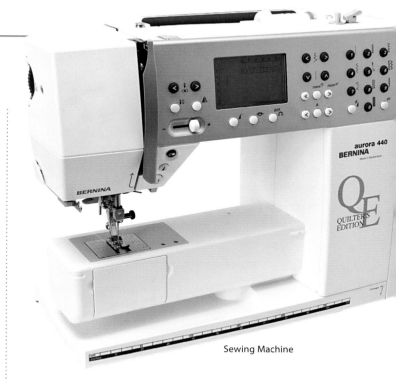

SCISSORS

Use 4″- to 5″-long shears with a sharp tip for clipping unwanted threads and fabric tips (bunny ears). Don't cut paper with fabric scissors, as doing so will quickly dull them.

PINS

Use extra-long, fine, glass-head pins. These are costly, but the less-expensive bargain brands are thick and will cause distortion when lining up seams. (I stock up when the good ones go on sale.)

THREAD

Use a quality cotton thread for piecing. Don't use decorative threads (such as metallic) or unusual fibers (such as rayon) for piecing. You can either match the thread color to your project or use a neutral gray or tan.

SEAM RIPPER

I hate to sound negative, but yes, even the seasoned quilter uses a seam ripper. Splurge and get yourself a quality one (you'll know by the price). Cheap, dull rippers will cause the fabric to stretch and will create more problems than they are worth.

Seam ripper

IRON

The one you have in your closet is probably just fine, but eventually you might want to purchase a super-hot steam iron. Correct pressing is very important in making a successful quilt.

Sewing Machine

SEWING MACHINE

Like cars, there are many different makes on the market. Eventually your sewing machine may be your biggest purchase. But for your first quilt, you simply need one that is in good working condition, with proper tension, an even stitch, and a good, sharp size 80 needle.

That's it! The rest of the tools are gravy. If you are like most quilters, however, one day you will look into your sewing room and realize the amount you paid for the contents could have put your firstborn through medical school. But shhh, don't tell anyone.

Thread

fabric

Choosing Fabrics

Quilting stores are found all over the world. It is in quilting stores that we can get the finest 100% cotton fabrics available. Different grades of cloth are used for the printed fabrics available to us. You want to use the best you can find. The less-expensive cottons are loosely woven with fewer threads per inch and will only cause you problems as they stretch and distort. Stay away from poly/cotton blends, which will shrink right before your eyes as you press the shapes.

As an avid fabric lover and collector, the thought of starting from scratch seems foreign to me. As I look back to my early days, I realize I did not really start to feel confident with fabric choices until after I had made several quilts. The fabric will dictate your quilt's mood or look. Each quilt in this book uses a different approach to fabric selection, which is briefly discussed at the onset of each project. Once you have decided what look you want, there are two vital rules to keep in mind.

- Always use light-, medium-, and dark-colored fabrics. Look how the second example below is composed only of mediums. It lacks the punch that the third example has. Medium fabrics are usually the most appealing, but force yourself to integrate both lights and darks. Using a combination of lights, mediums, and darks will make your quilt sparkle.

- Use printed fabrics that have variety in the character of the print. *Character of the print* refers to the design and scale of the print on the cloth. New quiltmakers often come to the craft with an image of what quilting prints should look like—that is, small calicos. However, when you use only one type of print, your quilt may look like it has the chicken pox. See how much more interesting the third example is than the first? This is because the third example not only has light, medium, and dark prints but also contains fabric with different characters of print, or visual texture. There are fabulous prints in delicious colors available to us. Never judge a fabric by how it looks on the bolt. We are not making clothing. Remember, when the fabric is cut up, it will look quite different.

tip ....

Try this trick: Take a 4˝ square of cardboard and cut a 2˝-square hole in the center. Position the cardboard over the fabric to see how the fabric will "read" when used in patchwork.

Be open to using fabrics that might make you feel uncomfortable. Remember, you aren't wearing the fabric; you are cutting it into little pieces and making a quilt. Experiment. That is how I grew to love and understand fabric relationships.

Don't use fabrics with all the same scale of print.

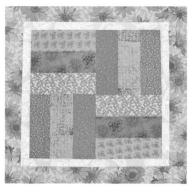

Don't use all the same value (lightness and darkness) of fabrics.

Do use fabrics with a variety of values and scale of prints.

Grain of the Fabric

When fabric is produced, threads are woven in two directions, creating a length and a width. This is called the straight of grain. If you cut diagonally across the grain (in triangle pieces), you are working on the bias. Bias edges must be sewn and pressed carefully, because they stretch easily. The long finished edges of the fabric are called the selvages. Always trim off the selvage edges—they cause distortion of the block and are difficult to hand quilt.

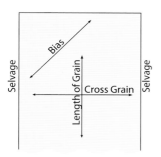

Grain of fabric

tip ....
When prewashing your fabric, unfold it completely before you put it in the washing machine, so you don't get a permanent fade mark along the original fold.

Preparing the Fabric

There are different schools of thought as to whether you should prewash your fabric. My philosophy is that you should, and here are three reasons.

- When the quilt is laundered, 100% cotton shrinks, causing puckers and distortion in the quilt.

- Darker dyes have been known to migrate to the lighter fabrics. This defines the expression "heartbreak."

- Fabric is treated with chemicals, and I don't think it is healthy to breathe or handle these chemicals over an extended period. I sometimes find myself wheezing when I decide to pass up prewashing.

tip ....
Always prewash darks and lights separately.

If you are working with a dark piece of fabric (reds and purples are extremely suspect), test your fabric by cutting a 2″ square and putting it in boiling water. If any color bleeds, wash your fabric in Retayne, Synthrapol, or a half-and-half solution of white vinegar and water. Dry and retest the fabric. If it still runs, repeat the solution process. If the fabric continues to run, throw it away. It could ruin your quilt.

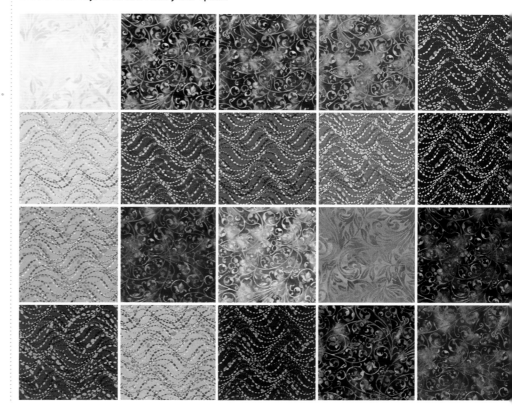

How to Make a Quilt

1. Make the blocks.

2. Sew the blocks together to create the quilt top.

3. Measure the quilt top.

4. Cut and attach the borders.

5. Layer the quilt top, batting, and backing.

6. Baste through all the layers.

7. Hand or machine quilt, attach the binding, and add a label.

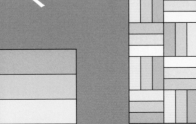

1.

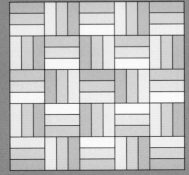

2.

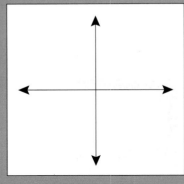

3.

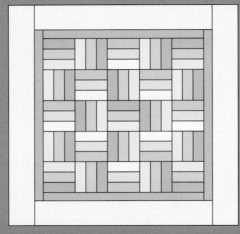

4.

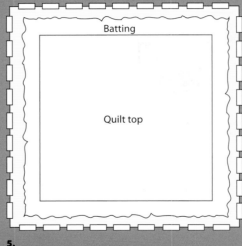

Batting

Quilt top

5.

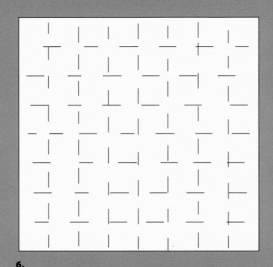

6.

7.

Decisions, Decisions, Decisions

Choose either the Rail Fence, Log Cabin Variation, Double Nine-Patch Variation, or Square Dance project to start with.

Rail Fence

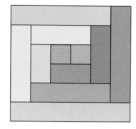

Log Cabin Variation

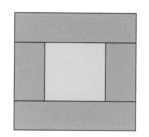

Square Dance

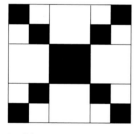

Double Nine-Patch Variation

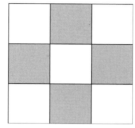

Nine-Patch

These patterns are made of shapes that are on the grain of the fabric. Therefore, they will not stretch or distort as you work with them.

After you have completed one or all of the projects using the blocks above, try your hand at the Friendship Star or Flying Geese blocks. Two of the project quilts in this book include the Flying Geese block. I have included two different methods for piecing the Flying Geese units. Try them both to see which one you prefer.

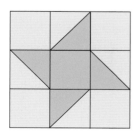

Friendship Star

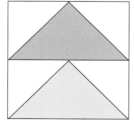

Flying Geese

These two blocks are a little more challenging because they have triangular shapes. Whenever you work with triangles, there is a risk of stretching the fabric as a result of bias edges. If you make a mistake or two, don't fret. This is a learning process. Enjoy it.

Rotary Cutting

I love rotary cutting. Please practice this technique on some scrap fabric before starting on your project.

Cutting Strips

1. When rotary cutting strips of fabric, fold the fabric selvage to selvage and then fold again, bringing the first fold up to match the selvages. Line up the straight of grain as much as possible. This folding will give you 4 layers of fabric to cut through. Line up the edge of the fabric with the cutting mat's grid.

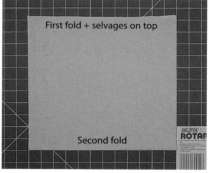

Fold the fabric.

2. Position the fabric on the mat, keeping all sides of the fabric in line with the mat's grid. (To prevent the fabric from being pulled out of alignment, keep the fabric from hanging off the edge of the table.)

3. Line up the vertical marks on the ruler with the grid on the cutting mat. To square up the raw edges, place the ruler ½″ over the raw edges of the fabric. Be careful to position your hand so that none of your fingers are hanging over the side of the ruler where you will be cutting. Rest your pinkie finger on the outside edge of the ruler. This not only will help protect your finger but will also keep the ruler from moving.

4. Place the rotary cutter blade right next to the ruler. Depress the safety latch of the cutter, exposing the blade; make a single pass (cutting away from your body) through the entire length of the fabric to remove the uneven raw edges.

Left-handed

Right-handed

5. Move the ruler over 3″ (to cut a 3″ strip), lining up the vertical 3″ mark on the ruler with the edge of the fabric. Line up one of the horizontal lines on the ruler with one of the horizontal grid lines on the mat and with the folded edge of the fabric. Cut the 3″ strip. Practice this a few times to get the hang of it. Follow this same process to cut the strips needed for your quilting projects.

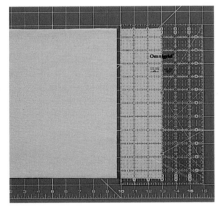

Left-handed

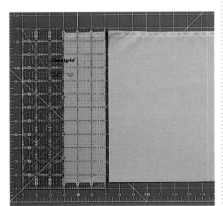

Right-handed

Position the ruler for rotary cutting a strip.

If the strip of fabric you are cutting is wider than your ruler, use the grid lines on your rotary mat to help you cut this wider strip.

tip · · · · · · · · · · · · · · · ·
Rotary cutters are very sharp. Retract the rotary cutter blade after every you cut. This is a good habit to develop from the start.

Cutting Squares, Rectangles, Half-Square Triangles, and Quarter-Square Triangles

6. Reposition the 3″-wide strip that you cut so that it is horizontal, on or parallel to one of the mat's grid lines. You can cut 4 squares or rectangles at a time (4 layers), or you can open the strip to cut 1 or 2 squares or rectangles at a time. Trim the edge of the fabric as you did in Steps 3 and 4, but only trim off about ⅛″ to square up the end of the strip.

7. To cut a 3″ × 3″ square, line up the vertical 3″ mark on the ruler with the edge of the fabric. Line up one of the horizontal lines on the ruler with one of the horizontal grid lines on the mat and with the folded edge of the fabric. Cut the square. Practice this a few times to get the hang of it. Rectangles are handled similarly. Repeat Steps 6 and 7 to cut all the squares and rectangles needed for your quilting project.

If the square of fabric you are cutting is wider than your ruler, use the grid lines on your rotary mat to help you cut this wider strip.

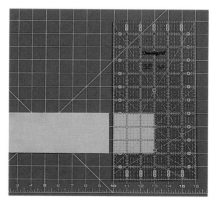

Left-handed

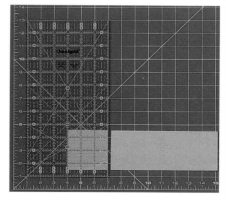

Right-handed

Position the ruler for rotary cutting a square.

8. Cut squares in half diagonally (corner to corner) to make half-square triangles. Use the 45° line on the ruler or the 45° line on the rotary mat to help make the cut more accurate.

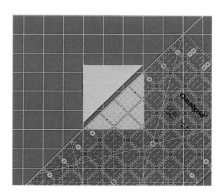

Left-handed

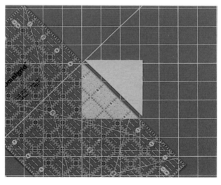

Right-handed

Position the ruler for rotary cutting a half-square triangle.

9. Cut squares in half diagonally again to make quarter-square triangles.

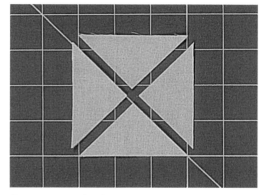

Quarter-square triangles

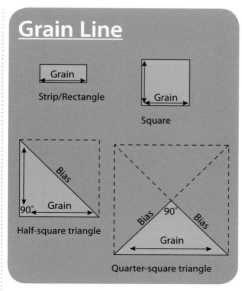

Grain Line

Grain

Strip/Rectangle

Grain

Square

Bias

90° Grain

Half-square triangle

Bias 90° Bias

Grain

Quarter-square triangle

Pinning

As you become acquainted with different quilters and quilting techniques, you will see that some people pin and some don't. I have found that the little time it takes to pin can determine the success of the block. Basically, you should pin where there are seams and intersections that need to line up. Here are a few guidelines:

1. When aligning seams that are pressed in opposite directions (like a Nine-Patch block, page 25), place a pin in both sides of the seam, no more than ⅛″ from the seamline.

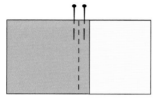

Pin seams pressed in opposite directions.

2. If you have a point of a triangle that needs to be positioned exactly (like the Flying Geese units, pages 37 and 40) follow these steps.

The Basics   13

A. Place the first pin in the wrong side of unit A (exactly at the intersection), inserting it into the right side of unit B (exactly at the ¼" seam allowance). Press the head of the pin firmly through both layers.

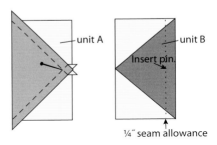

Pin the point of the triangle to align exactly.

B. While holding the pin firmly in place, place the second and third pins on either side of the intersection, no more than ⅛" from the first pin. Let the first pin dangle loosely.

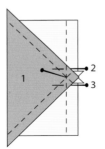

Insert second and third pins.

C. Stitch so that the piece requiring the exact point is on top. As you approach the intersection, remove the first pin at the last second and let the sewing machine needle drop into that hole. If your sewing machine doesn't sew over pins easily, remove the second and third pins right before you stitch over them.

I have found this to be a great technique, and I encourage you to develop this habit.

Stitching

Set the stitch length on your machine just long enough so that your seam ripper slides nicely under the stitches. This is about 10–12 stitches per inch. Back-tacking is not necessary for the projects in this book, because all the seam ends will be enclosed by other seams.

¼" Seam Allowance

When piecing a quilt top, you always use a ¼" seam allowance. Cutting instructions in this book include that seam allowance. Many machines have an exact ¼" foot. If yours does, you are home free. If not, put your clear plastic rotary cutting ruler under the sewing machine needle and drop the presser foot, then manually ease the needle down on top of the ¼" mark. Take a thin piece of masking tape and mark the ¼" mark on the throat plate, using the edge of the ruler as your guide.

As you sew the pieces together, use this piece of tape as your seam guide. This is an extremely important step for ensuring accuracy. Take the time to understand your machine's ¼". My kids' term "close enough" will only reward you with yards of frustration.

tip ·······················

To check your ¼", Sally Collins of Walnut Creek, California, recommends that you cut 2 strips of fabric each 1" × 3½". Sew the 2 strips together along one 3½" side, press, and measure. The sewn unit should be 1½" wide. If not, try again until you find your machine's perfect ¼".

Seam Ripping

On occasion, you will want to pick out a seam. Cut every third stitch on one side of the fabric, then lift the thread off the other side of the fabric.

If you have two bias edges sewn together, as in the Flying Geese block (pages 37 and 40), consider throwing the unit away and starting over. The chance of stretching the bias pieces when removing the stitches is almost 100%. If the pieces do stretch, they won't line up and won't fit properly when stitched to the next section.

Pressing

Pressing is a very important area of quiltmaking. Many beginners approach the pressing portion of quiltmaking as if they were ironing the weekly laundry. Old habits are hard to break, but you must learn this new technique if you want to have super-looking quilts. The following tips are for pieced units.

- Press on a firm surface (an ironing board with a single pad). Seams are usually pressed in either one direction or another (not open). Press in the direction indicated by the arrows in the instructions; first on the wrong side, then on the right side. This helps the seams to align in your block construction.

Press in the direction of the arrows.

- The final pressing is on the right side of the fabric. This will prevent tucks from being pressed into the sewn seams.

Settings

The blocks in all the projects in this book are placed in a straight set to form the quilt top. A straight set is the easiest, and therefore the best, way to begin. The blocks are positioned with the sides vertical and horizontal to the quilt's edges, not diagonal (setting them diagonal is called "on point" in quilter's language).

First arrange the blocks in a pleasing manner. Then sew the blocks into rows and press. Once the rows are sewn, sew each row to the next row. Press as the arrows indicate.

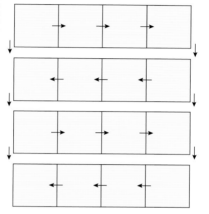

Pressing for straight setting

On-point setting

Borders

1. Measure your sewn and pressed top across the center of the quilt, from top to bottom and from one side to the other. Compare your measurements with the measurements in the instructions. If your ¼" seam allowance is off, this is where the difference will show up. If your quilt top measurements match the measurements in the project instructions, cut your border strips the lengths provided.

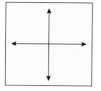

Measure across the center.

2. If your quilt top measurements do not match the measurements in the instructions, cut the top and bottom border strips the length of your quilt top from side to side by the border width given in the project instructions. Find the center of the quilt top and the center of the top border strip by folding them in half and pinning them together, right sides together. Pin the ends of the border strip to the corners of the quilt top and then pin every 2". Sew and press, following the pressing arrows. Repeat for the bottom border.

3. Measure your quilt top from top to bottom across the center, including the borders. Cut the side border strips this length by the width given in the project instructions. Pin and sew as in Step 2 to attach the side borders. Press.

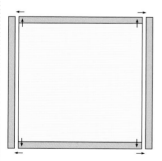

Inner border

4. Repeat Steps 1–3 for the outer border.

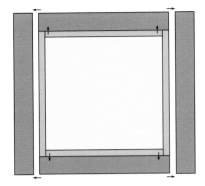

Outer border

note

If your quilt is longer vertically than it is horizontally, as in *Friendship Star Quilt* (page 32), cut and attach the side borders first, then the top and bottom borders. This will use shorter strips and save fabric.

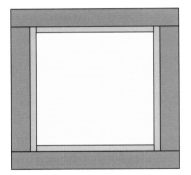

Borders for vertical quilt

When your quilt top is complete, you must decide on the next phase of your quilting journey. Following are the final considerations you need to make.

Planning the Quilting

Quilting is the act of stitching all three layers together. It is now time to consider how you are going to quilt the top—by machine or by hand. I prefer hand quilting, because it lends a softer, homespun look. I would suggest that you take the time to try hand quilting. I have always enjoyed this part of the process and find that hand-quilted quilts have a special look. However, it does require a significant amount of time, and if this is a quilt that kids are going to drag around or that is for a bed that the dogs jump on (I know about these things), you should try machine quilting. Your decision should be determined by the look you want to achieve and/or by the destination of the quilt.

Quilting Design

For your first project, I recommend that you keep the quilting as simple as possible. You might want to start by quilting in the ditch. This is done by quilting as close as possible to the sewn seam on the side without the seam allowance. It is a great way for a beginner to start. Your stitches will be hidden, giving you time to perfect your quilting technique. I also love using simple grids that cover the entire surface. If you look carefully at the projects in this book, you will see that I also used some basic quilting designs from clear plastic templates (available at your local quilt store, a quilt show, or a quilt magazine) to add interest. Later in your quilting career you might want to take a class that teaches you how to create your own quilting designs. For now, in the ditch, basic grid, or a simple template will do the job.

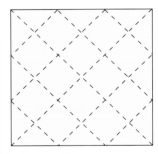

Quilting a grid

MARKING TOOLS

I usually use a silver Verithin pencil or white powdered chalk. The silver pencil stays on longer, whereas the chalk comes off easily. Never use a regular graphite pencil, as it may not come out.

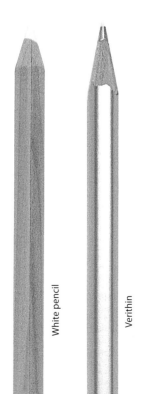

White pencil

Verithin

Before marking the entire top, always test the marking tool on your fabric first to make sure the marks come out.

Narrow ¼″ masking tape is a good way to mark straight lines. Place the tape where you want a straight line of quilting stitches and sew your stitches right next to (not through) the tape.

Creating a Basic Grid

All the quilt tops in this book are based on 6″ blocks. Make marks at 2″ increments around the edge of the pieced blocks and then use your ruler to lightly draw lines with your marking tool.

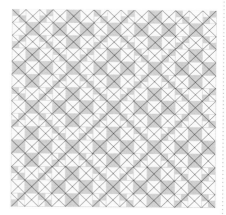

Quilting grid marked on Nine-Patch Variation (page 24)

If you decide to incorporate a stencil, as seen in the Rail Fence border place the stencil on top and trace the template design.

The Quilt Sandwich

Backing

All the basic projects in this book are 42″ wide or less. This eliminates the problem of piecing the backing together. If you follow the instructions is Appendix A and find that your quilt top is wider than 42″, you will have to sew sections of the backing fabric together to create a wide enough piece of fabric to cover the quilt top. It's OK to use different cotton prints for one backing. Choosing the fabrics for the backing can be as much fun as deciding on the fabric for the front of the quilt. Here are a few things to keep in mind:

- Always prewash and cut off the selvage edges before piecing the fabric together. It is difficult to hand quilt through the selvages, and the seams won't lie flat.

- If your quilt top has a lot of white in it, use light colors for the backing, so they don't show through the batting to the front.

- Always make the backing a few inches larger than the top on all four sides, in case your quilt top shifts during quilting.

tip ·

Never use a sheet or a piece of decorator fabric for the backing. This fabric has a high thread count and is difficult to hand quilt.

Batting

For hand quilting, I recommend starting with a low-loft polyester batting. It makes the quilting stitch much easier to learn.

For machine quilting, I recommend that you use 100% cotton batting. Make sure you follow the instructions on the package if it needs to be prewashed.

Layering

Depending on the size of my project, I either work on a tabletop (small quilt) or on my nonloop carpet (large quilt). First you must place the quilt backing wrong side up on your working area. Either tape it down (tabletop) or pin using T pins (carpet), working from the center of each side to the corners. Keep the fabric grain straight and make sure the backing is stretched taut. No bubbles or ripples are acceptable; otherwise, you will have folds and tucks in the back of your finished quilt.

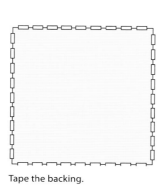

Tape the backing.

Carefully unroll the batting and smooth it on top of the backing. Trim the batting to the same size as the backing. Smooth the quilt top onto the batting, right side up. The quilt top is a few inches smaller than the backing and batting on all four sides.

Basting

The purpose of basting is to hold the layers together and prevent them from shifting during quilting. The basting will be removed when the quilting is finished.

FOR HAND QUILTING

Using a long needle and thread, knot one end of the thread and take large stitches through all three layers.

tip . . . .

Never baste with a colored thread, because the dye might migrate on to the fabric.

Don't bother knotting the other end of the thread. When it's time to remove the basting you can just give the knotted end of the thread a little tug, and it will pull out.

I like to baste in a grid pattern (about every 4″), so there is an even amount of basting throughout the quilt.

Baste in a grid.

Never skimp on this part of the process. It will only cause disaster down the road, because your quilt layers may slip and move during the quilting process.

FOR MACHINE QUILTING

Unlike hand quilting, you will pin baste every 3″ with safety pins. Pin evenly across the quilt, staying away from where the quilting stitches will be sewn. Special safety pins have been made for machine quilting. These pins are small (size #0 or #1) and are all the same size.

Quilting

Hand Quilting

For hand quilting you will need:

HOOP/FRAME

I recommend starting with a 16″ round quilting hoop. Never use an embroidery hoop; they aren't strong enough. A frame that sits on the floor provides excellent tension control and keeps your quilt flat and square. However, it is a substantial investment, and you must first find out whether you enjoy hand quilting. You will know when it's time to invest in a quilting frame. When you do, shop at the quilt shows and shops and make sure the frame has the following three components: excellent tension control, stability, and ease of assembly.

Hoop

THIMBLE

Forget grandma's thimble from her treasured sewing box. Get a thimble that is made especially for hand quilting. Quilting thimbles have deep indentations that hold the needle and prevent the needle from slipping on the thimble's surface.

THREAD

Several brands are available; make sure that the thread you buy is made especially for hand quilting. It will be marked as quilting thread on the end of the spool. Quilting thread is a little heavier than regular sewing thread.

NEEDLES

Quilting needles are called "betweens." Start with a #9; as you learn the stitch, try a higher number. The higher the number, the smaller the needle. I use a #11.

Hand-Quilting Stitches

Hand quilting is done with a simple running stitch.

To get started:

1. Position the basted quilt in your hoop, with the quilt top facing up. *Always work from the center of the quilt to the outside edge to keep the layers smooth and to avoid tucks.* Make sure that the back is as taut as the top; then loosen all three layers just a little (by pushing inside the hoop with your hand), so the needle can be easily manipulated.

2. Put a small single knot in the thread. Insert the needle through the quilt top and batting (not into the backing) an inch away from where you want to start quilting. Bring it up where you will start quilting. Gently pull on the thread, running your thumbnail over the knot to help pop the knot between the layers. This is called "burying" the knot.

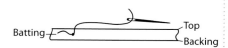

Bury the knot.

tip ·····················

A thimble is a must. Although you might be uncomfortable working with one at first, it will become your most valuable tool. Typically, the thimble is worn on the middle finger. The thimble indentations hold the blunt end of the needle as you stitch.

3. Place your hand with the thimble on top of the quilt and your other hand under the quilt. Hold the needle straight up and down between the thumb and ring finger.

Left-handed

Right-handed

4. When you feel the prick of the needle on your underneath finger, pivot the needle tip back up. Push down with your thumb in front of the hill where the stitch is about to be taken. Push the needle through the layers, creating the first stitch.

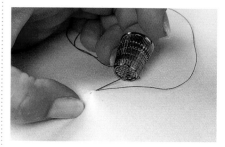

Left-handed

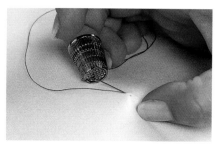

Right-handed

5. Repeat this process until you have a few stitches on the needle. This is called the rocking stitch. Pull the needle and thread until the thread is taut.

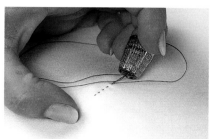

Left-handed

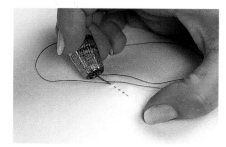

Right-handed

6. When you come to the end of your thread, create another single knot and bury it between the 3 layers. Pull the remaining amount of thread up and carefully snip off the end.

7. Practice making your stitches even in size.

Bury the knot and cut the thread.

Machine Quilting

Machine quilting is an art form of its own. With practice, machine quilting can be a beautiful addition to your quilts.

For machine quilting you will need:

WALKING FOOT

When you quilt using a sewing machine, the layers of fabric and batting will not feed in evenly, causing tucks on the backside of the quilt. A walking foot helps solve this problem.

Walking foot

THREAD

Use 100% cotton thread in a color that blends with the quilt top (usually a medium color).

Thread

Machine-Quilting Stitches

Support your quilt on all sides. Quilt on a large table. You can use an ironing board, adjusted to your table height, on the left-hand side and perpendicular to the table. Ideally, your sewing machine should be recessed into your table to create a level surface.

1. To start machine quilting, stitch in the ditch or on a grid (see page 17). Reduce your stitch length almost (but not exactly) to 0 and lower the presser foot right over the spot where you plan to start quilting. Holding on to the top thread, take one complete stitch, so the needle returns to its highest position.

2. While raising the presser foot, gently tug the top thread to pull the loop of bobbin thread to the quilt surface. Pull the end of the bobbin thread through to the top.

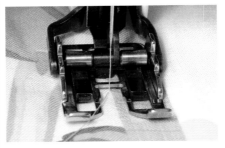 

Take one complete stitch, ending with the needle at its highest position.

Pull the top thread to bring the loop of bobbin thread to surface.

3. Insert the needle into the exact spot where the bobbin thread came up. Hold the threads to the side as you take 1 or 2 stitches.

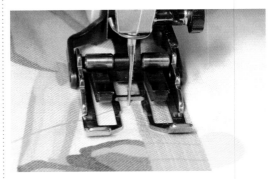

Insert needle and take 1 or 2 stitches.

4. Gradually increase the stitch length (approximately 10–12 stitches per inch) with 6–8 stitches.

5. Continue stitching to complete your machine quilting. When you're ready to end a row of stitching, gradually decrease the stitch length back to almost 0 and stitch a few more stitches.

Transition the length of your stitches to begin and end your quilting.

Stitch one row in each direction (closest to the center), both vertically and horizontally, to secure the 3 layers. Then work from the center out as you quilt the remaining lines. After the center quilting is complete, stitch in-the-ditch around the border seams; add quilting in the border if desired. Look for quilting designs that are designed for machine quilting.

Binding

Trim the batting and backing even with the edges of the quilt top. The binding holds all three layers together and often gets the most abuse when a quilt is loved and used.

1. Cut 2¼″ × 42″ strips. Trim them to the width of the quilt from side to side, plus 1″ for trimming. If your quilt is more than 42″ wide, you will need to piece strips together to get the desired length. Create this union with a seam that is on an angle, as shown, to prevent a big lump in the binding.

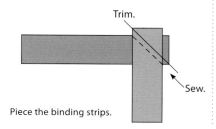

Piece the binding strips.

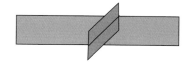

Trim the seams.

2. Fold wrong sides together and press lengthwise.

Fold and press.

3. On the top edge of the front of the quilt, line up the raw edges of the binding with the raw edge of the quilt. Let the binding extend ½″ past the corners of the quilt. Sew using a ¼″ seam allowance. Do this on the top and bottom edges of the quilt.

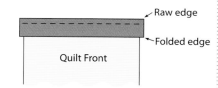

Attach the binding to the front of the quilt.

4. Flip the finished edge of the binding over the raw edge of the quilt and slipstitch the binding to the back of the quilt. Trim the ends even with the edge of the quilt, as shown.

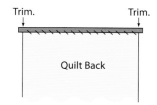

Stitch the binding and trim.

5. Cut 2 strips 2¼″ × 42″. For the 2 remaining sides of the quilt, measure the length of the quilt from top to bottom. Trim the strips to this measurement plus ½″ for turning under. Sew on the binding strips to the front of the quilt fold over the end of the binding to create a finished edge before folding the binding to the back. Slipstitch down.

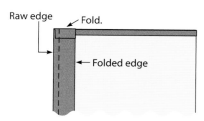

Attach the side binding.

As you travel into the world of quilting, please always keep this in mind—there is not one definitive way to make a quilt. Expose yourself to as many different approaches as possible. Take classes. Soon you will become comfortable with what works for you. Check out the local quilting guild. You will meet great people there. And remember, always sign, date, and document your project on the quilt back with a permanent marking pen designed specifically for fabric.

Quiltmaking is a journey both men and women have loved for generations. We all started at the same place, so there's no need to feel intimidated by a lack of experience. Welcome to the wonderful world and people of quiltmaking!

Alex Anderson, QUILTMAKER

Rail Fence Quilt

Quilts made with pastel floral prints are perennial favorites with quilters. A colorful, large-scale flowered fabric made the perfect border—and focus fabric—for this Rail Fence- design. I simply used the soft, feminine colors to guide my other fabric choices.

This wallhanging is 41½″ × 41½″ and is made up of twenty-five 6″ finished Rail Fence blocks. Pieced and machine quilted by Pam Vieira-McGinnis.

Fabric Requirements

Fabric requirements are based on 42″ fabric width.

- Focus fabric: ¾ yard for outer border
- Pink: ¼ yard each of 3 different fabrics for blocks
- Green: ¼ yard each of 3 different fabrics for blocks
- Lavender: ¼ yard each of 3 different fabrics for blocks
- Print: ¼ yard for inner border
- Binding: ⅜ yard
- Backing: 1¼ yards

Please read The Basics (pages 11–22) before starting.

Rail Fence Blocks

Rail Fence block

Cutting

From each of the 9 fabrics:

- Cut 2 strips 2½" × 42" (pages 11–12) for blocks.

Piecing and Pressing

1. Sew 1 of each of the 3 different pink strips together (page 14). The strip set should measure 6½" wide. Make 2 strip sets. Press as the arrows indicate.

Sew the strips together and press.

2. Repeat for the green and lavender fabrics. You will now have 2 sewn 6½" strips of each color family.

3. Trim one end straight (pages 11–12).

4. Cut each sewn unit into 6½" blocks (see pages 12–13). You will need 8 pink, 8 lavender, and 9 green blocks.

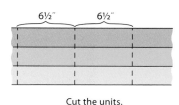

Cut the units.

tip ···

This process is called strip piecing.

5. Lay out your blocks as shown. Note that they are in a straight set (page 15).

6. Sew the blocks into rows and press. Sew the rows together. Refer to page 15 for pressing.

Your quilt top should measure 30½" × 30½". If it does, use the instructions below to cut and attach the inner and outer border strips. If it doesn't, see page 15 to measure and cut the correct border lengths for your quilt top.

INNER BORDER

7. Cut 2 strips 1½" × 30½" for the top and bottom and 2 strips 1½" × 32½" for the sides.

8. Sew on the inner border (first the shorter top and bottom strips, then the longer side strips). Refer to page 15 for pressing.

OUTER BORDER

9. Cut 2 strips 5" × 32½" for the top and bottom and 2 strips 5" × 41½" for the sides.

10. Sew on the outer border (first the shorter top and bottom strips, then the longer side strips). Press.

Yay! I knew you could do it. Now it's time to decide how to quilt and finish it (pages 16–21).

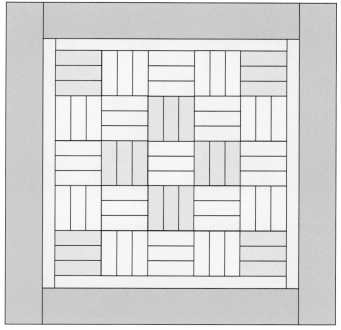

Rail Fence quilt

Nine-Patch Variation Quilt

I never tire of working with toile, as the restrained palette makes for a timeless quilt. When working with a monochromatic (one-color) color scheme, make sure to include a full range of values, as I have done here with white (light), black-and-white toile (medium), and black (dark).

This wallhanging is 30½″ × 30½″ and is made up of twelve 6″ finished Nine-Patch blocks and thirteen 6″ finished Nine-Patch Variation blocks. Pieced and machine quilted by Pam Vieira-McGinnis.

Fabric Requirements

Fabric requirements are based on 42″ fabric width.

- Black: ⅓ yard for blocks

- Black-and-white print: ⅓ yard for blocks

- White: 1 yard for blocks

- Binding: ⅓ yard

- Backing: 1 yard

Please read The Basics (pages 11–21) before starting.

Nine-Patch Blocks

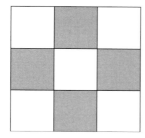

Nine-Patch block

Cutting

Black-and-white print:

- Cut 4 strips 2½″ × 42″ (pages 11–12) for blocks.

White:

- Cut 5 strips 2½″ × 42″ for blocks.

Piecing and Pressing

Press as the arrows indicate (page 15).

1. Set A: Sew a white strip to each long edge of a black and white strip. Repeat to make a second Set A. Press.

2. Cut Sets A into 24 segments 2½″ wide (same technique as for cutting squares, pages 12–13).

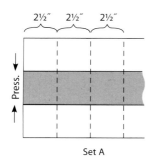

Set A

3. Set B: Sew a black-and-white print strip to each long edge of a white strip. Press.

4. Cut Set B into 12 segments 2½″ wide.

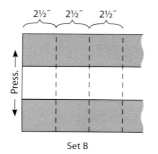

Set B

5. Arrange and sew Segments A and B into 12 Nine-Patch blocks as shown, matching the seams and pinning (page 13).

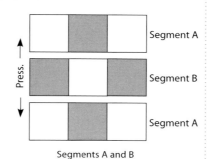

Segment A
Segment B
Segment A

Segments A and B

Double Nine-Patch Variation Blocks

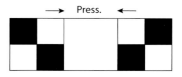

Double Nine-Patch Variation block

Cutting

Black:

- Cut 4 strips 1½″ × 42″ and 1 strip 2½″ × 42″ for blocks.

White:

- Cut 4 strips 1½″ × 42″ and 4 strips 2½″ × 42″ for blocks.

Piecing and Pressing

6. Set C: Sew together pairs of the black and white 1½″ strips. Press as the arrows indicate.

7. Cut Sets C into 104 segments 1½″ wide.

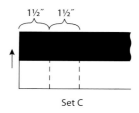

Set C

8. Sew together Segments C in pairs, as shown, to make 52 Four-Patch blocks. Press as the arrows indicate.

Four-Patch block

9. Cut 26 white 2½″ squares from 2 of the strips.

10. Arrange the Four-Patch blocks and the white squares as shown; sew. Press.

Press.

Segment C unit

11. Set D: Sew 2 white and 1 black 2½″ strips, as shown. Press. Cut into 13 segments 2½″ wide.

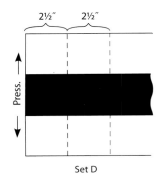

2½″   2½″

Press.

Set D

Segment D

12. Arrange and sew Segment C units and Segment D together. Press.

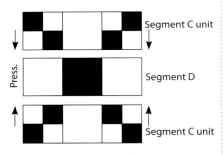

Press.

Segment C unit

Segment D

Segment C unit

Arrange, sew, and press.

tip · · · · · · · · · · · · · · · ·

This is called strip piecing and using a block combination.

13. Lay out your Nine-Patch and Double Nine-Patch Variation blocks as shown. Note that they are in a straight set.

14. Sew the blocks into rows and press. Sew the rows together (page 15). Refer to page 15 for pressing.

Great job! I hope you love your Nine-Patch Variation quilt as much as I love mine. Please turn to pages 16–21 for additional information to help you finish up your little treasure.

Nine-Patch Variation quilt

Square Dance Quilt

Oh, how we quilters love batiks! Some are subtle tone on tones, while others are vibrant and multicolored. Feel free to experiment with the wide range of combinations and variations. In this quilt, the border fabric acted as my color guide.

This quilt measures 40½″ × 46½″ and is made up of thirty 6″ finished Square Dance blocks. Pieced and machine quilted by Pam Vieira-McGinnis.

Fabric Requirements

Fabric requirements are based on 42″ fabric width.

- Assorted coordinating pink, green, purple, yellow, and tan batiks (A): ½ yard total for blocks

- Assorted coordinating pink, green, purple, yellow, and tan batiks (B): 1 yard total for blocks

- Pink (C): ⅓ yard for inner border

- Multicolored print (D): ⅔ yard for outer border

- Binding: ⅜ yard

- Backing: 2¾ yards

Please read The Basics (pages 11–21) before starting.

Square Dance Blocks

Square Dance block

Cutting

Fabric A:

- Cut a total of 30 squares 3½″ × 3½″ for block centers.

Fabric B:

- Cut a total of 60 rectangles 2″ × 3½″ in matching pairs for block bars.

- Cut a total of 60 rectangles 2″ × 6½″ in matching pairs for block bars.*

Cut 1 pair to match each pair of 2″ × 3½″ Fabric B rectangles.

Piecing and Pressing

1. Sew a 3½″ Fabric A square between 2 matching 2″ × 3½″ Fabric B rectangles. Press. Make 30.

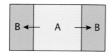

Make 30.

2. Sew matching 2″ × 6½″ Fabric B rectangles to the top and bottom of each unit from Step 1. Press. Make 30.

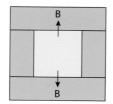

Make 30.

3. Lay out your blocks as shown. Note that they are in a straight set (page 15).

4. Sew the blocks into rows and press. Sew the rows together (page 15). Refer to page 15 for pressing.

Your quilt top should measure 30½″ × 36½″. If it does, use the instructions below to cut and attach the inner and outer border strips. If it doesn't, see pages 15–16 to measure and cut the correct border lengths for your quilt top.

INNER BORDER

5. Cut 2 strips 2″ × 36½″ for the sides and 2 strips 2″ × 33½″ for the top and bottom.

6. Sew on the inner border (first the sides, then the top and bottom). Refer to page 15 for pressing.

OUTER BORDER

7. Cut 2 strips 4″ × 39½″ for the sides and 2 strips 4″ × 40½″ for the top and bottom.

8. Sew on the outer border (first the sides, then the top and bottom). Press.

Yay! I knew you could do it. Now it's time to decide how to quilt and finish it (pages 16–21).

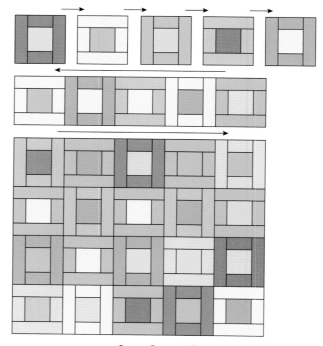

Square Dance quilt

Log Cabin Variation Quilt

There are several variations of the Log Cabin block. Typically, one half of the logs are light and the other half are dark. The Log Cabin Variation block used in this project is an off-center log cabin since there is not an equal number of light and dark logs.

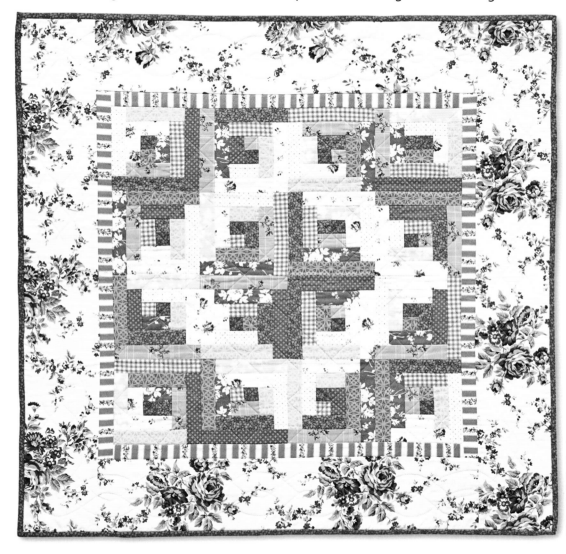

This quilt measures 36½″ × 36½″ and is made up of sixteen 6″ finished Log Cabin Variation blocks. Pieced and machine quilted by Pam Vieira-McGinnis.

Fabric Requirements

Fabric requirements are based on 42″ fabric width.

- Print #1: 1 yard for outer border

- Red: ⅓ yard for chimneys and binding

- Darks: ¼ yard each of 6 different fabrics

- Lights: ¼ yard each of 4 different fabrics

- Print #2: ¼ yard for inner border

- Backing: 1¼ yards

Please read The Basics (pages 11–21) before starting.

tip

Focus Fabric: Let the colors in your main print dictate the look of the quilt.

Log Cabin Variation

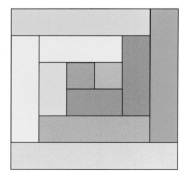

Log Cabin Variation block

Cutting

Red:

- Cut 1 strip 1½″ wide; cut into 16 squares 1½″ × 1½″ for chimneys.

Darks:

- Cut 3 strips 1½″ × 42″ of each dark fabric for dark logs.

Lights:

- Cut 3 strips 1½″ × 42″ of each light fabric for light logs.

Piecing and Pressing

The following instructions are for one Log Cabin block.

1. Sew a red chimney square onto a dark strip. Press as the arrows indicate. Using your rotary cutter and ruler, trim the strip even with the edges of the red square (Unit A).

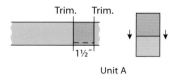

Unit A

2. Sew a different dark strip onto Unit A. Press and trim to form Unit B.

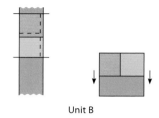

Unit B

3. Rotate the block so the previously sewn log is at the bottom. Sew a light strip onto Unit B. Press and trim to make Unit C.

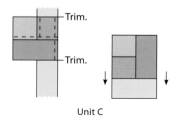

Unit C

4. Rotate the block as in Step 3. Sew a different light strip onto Unit C. Press and trim to make Unit D.

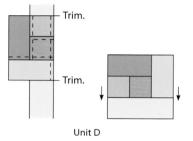

Unit D

The key to a Log Cabin block is to keep working your way around the block clockwise with this pattern in mind: chimney, dark, dark, light, light, dark, dark, light, light, dark, dark. Sew 16 blocks.

tip ·····················

Always keep the previously sewn log at the bottom.

5. Lay out your blocks as shown. Note that they are in a straight set (page 15).

note ·················

Because of the strong diagonal movement of color, you can get many different looks by rotating the blocks. Once all your blocks are completed, feel free to play with the arrangement before you sew them together. You might like your set (arrangement) better than the one I decided on.

6. Sew the blocks into rows and press. Sew the rows together. Refer to page 15 for pressing.

Your quilt top should measure 24½˝ × 24½˝. If it does, use the instructions below to cut and attach the inner and outer border strips. If it doesn't, see pages 15–16 to measure and cut the correct border lengths for your quilt top.

INNER BORDER

7. Cut 2 strips 1½˝ × 24½˝ for the top and bottom and 2 strips 1½˝ × 26½˝ for the sides.

8. Sew on the inner border (first the shorter top and bottom strips, then the longer side strips). Refer to page 15 for pressing.

OUTER BORDER

9. Cut 2 strips 5½˝ × 26½˝ for the top and bottom and 2 strips 5½˝ × 36½˝ for the sides.

10. Sew on the outer border (first the shorter top and bottom strips, then the longer side strips). Press.

11. Please refer to pages 16–21 to finish your wonderful Log Cabin Variation quilt.

Log Cabin Variation quilt

Friendship Star Quilt

My heart leapt when I found this incredible pink-and-coral border fabric. I used a variety of green background prints for the blocks, and not all of them match the border fabric exactly. Not only is this okay, it makes the design more interesting.

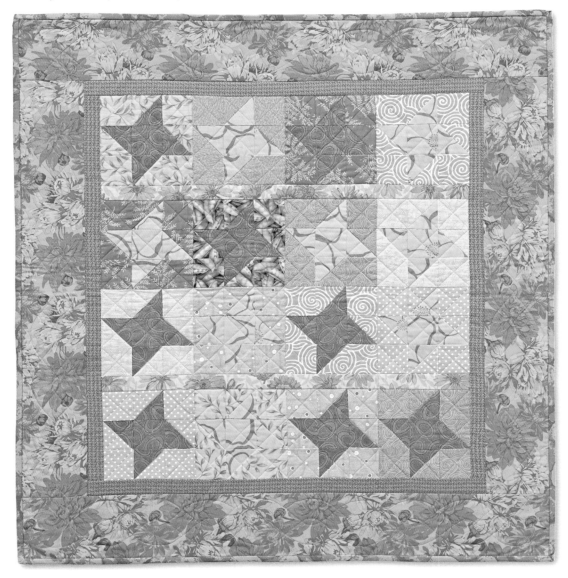

This quilt measures 34½″ × 36½″ and is made up of sixteen 6″ finished Friendship Star blocks. Pieced and machine quilted by Pam Vieira-McGinnis.

Fabric Requirements

Fabric requirements are based on 42″ fabric width.

- Focus fabric: 1 yard for outer border

- Orange prints: ¼ yard each of 2 different fabrics for stars

- Green prints: ⅛ yard each of 9 different fabrics for block backgrounds

- Print #1: ⅛ yard for sashing

- Print #2: ¼ yard for inner border

- Binding: ⅜ yard

- Backing: 1¼ yards

Please read The Basics (pages 11–21) before starting.

Now it's time to tackle triangles! The Friendship Star is basically a Nine-Patch block (page 25) with half-square triangles at the top, bottom, and sides. Half-square triangles are easy to work with. My only caution is that you have now entered the world of exposed, cut bias edges. Here are two rules to keep in mind when working with triangles:

- Never press the fabric shape once it has been cut and before it has been sewn. You stand a big chance of stretching the exposed, cut bias edge.

- Never pull the units through the sewing machine as you stitch them together; this can stretch the shape. Let your machine do the work for you, not your hands.

Friendship Star Block

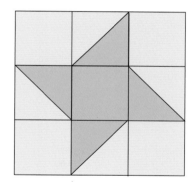

Friendship Star block

Cutting

Orange prints:

- Cut 8 squares 2½″ × 2½″ from each fabric (16 total) for star centers.

- Cut 16 squares 2⅞″ × 2⅞″ from each fabric (32 total), then cut in half diagonally for star points.

Green prints:

- Cut 8 squares 2½″ × 2½″ from each fabric (need 64 total) for block corners. You will have extra squares to play with for color placement.

- Cut 4 squares 2⅞″ × 2⅞″ from each fabric (need 32 total), then cut in half diagonally for block background.

Cutting half-square triangles

Piecing and Pressing

1. Sew an orange star triangle to a green background triangle along the long side. Press as the arrows indicate. Repeat 3 more times. Trim bunny ears.

Star points

2. Lay out and sew the block as shown. Press as the arrows indicate. Sew 16 blocks.

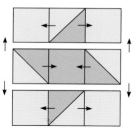

Friendship Star

3. Lay out your blocks as shown on page 34. Note that they are in a straight set (page 15).

4. Sew together each row of 4 stars, being sure to match the seams and pin. Press as the arrows indicate.

PRINT #1 SASHING

5. Your rows should measure 24½″ wide. If they do, cut 2 strips 1½″ × 24½″. If they don't, cut the sashing strips the measurement of your rows.

6. Insert the 2 rows of sashing and sew the rows together. Press as the arrows indicate.

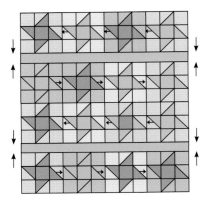

Add sashing.

tip . . . .

When assembling vertical rows of blocks that include sashing, make sure to line up the blocks, even though the sashing is in between.

Your quilt top should measure 24½″ × 26½″. If it does, use the instructions that follow to cut and attach the inner and outer border strips. If it doesn't, see pages 15–16 to measure and cut the correct border lengths for your quilt top.

INNER BORDER

This quilt is a rectangle. To conserve fabric, the side borders are sewn on before the top and bottom borders.

7. Cut 4 strips 1½″ × 26½″ from Print #2.

8. Sew on the inner border (first the side strips, then the top and bottom). Refer to page 15 for pressing.

OUTER BORDER

9. Cut 2 strips 4½″ × 28½″ for the sides and 2 strips 4½″ × 34½″ for the top and bottom borders.

10. Sew on the outer border (first the shorter side strips, then the top and bottom). Press.

You did it! Welcome to the wonderful world of stars. They are my all-time favorites. I hope you learn to love them as I do. Now it's time to quilt and finish your Friendship Star (pages 16–21).

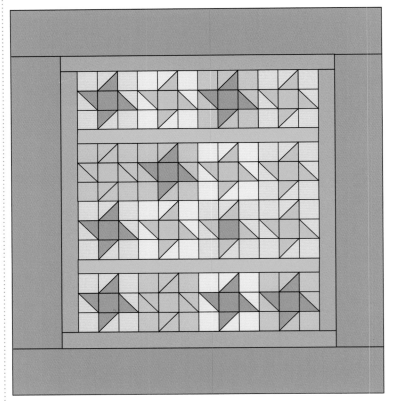

Friendship Star quilt

Flying Geese Quilt

Once again, a multicolored border fabric guided the fabric choices for my quilt. In this case, the border fabric is a one-way print. Keep your eye out for these sometimes-subtle fabrics: you may need to purchase extra to accommodate their directional nature. Piece the leftovers with other fabrics to use on the back.

This quilt measures 34½″ × 34½″ and contains sixteen 6″ finished Flying Geese blocks. Pieced and machine quilted by Pam Vieira-McGinnis.

Fabric Requirements

Fabric requirements are based on 42″ fabric width.

- Focus fabric: 1 yard for outer border

- Green: ¼ yard each of 2 different fabrics for geese

- Blue: ¼ yard each of 2 different fabrics for geese

- White: ½ yard for geese background

- Print: ¼ yard for inner border

- Binding: ⅜ yard

- Backing: 1¼ yards

Please read The Basics (pages 11–21) before starting.

Each Flying Geese block is made up of two Flying Geese units, using quarter-square triangles and half-square triangles. Although the triangles both have 45°, 45°, and 90° angle corners, they are very different. The half-square triangle has two edges that are on the straight of grain, while the quarter-square triangle has only one edge that is on the straight of grain. This difference is very important—when sewn, the outside edge of the block should always be on the straight of grain to avoid unnecessary stretching.

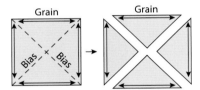

Grain for Flying Geese units

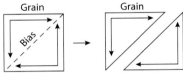

Half-square triangles

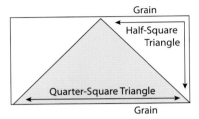

Quarter-square triangles

The difference between a half-square and a quarter-square triangle is the location of the bias edges.

Remember, when working with triangles:

- Never press the fabric shape once it has been cut and before it has been sewn. You stand a big chance of stretching the exposed cut bias edge.

- Never pull the units through the sewing machine as you stitch them together; this can stretch the shapes. Let your machine do the work for you, not your hands.

Flying Geese

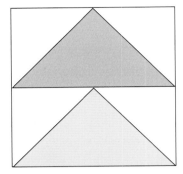

Flying Geese block

Cutting

Green:

- Cut 2 squares 7¼˝ × 7¼˝ from each green fabric, then cut in half diagonally twice for geese. Yields 16 quarter-square triangles.

Blue:

- Cut 2 squares 7¼˝ × 7¼˝ from each blue fabric, then cut in half diagonally twice for geese. Yields 16 quarter-square triangles.

White background:

- Cut 32 squares 3⅞˝ × 3⅞˝, then cut in half diagonally for geese background. Yields 64 half-square triangles.

Piecing and Pressing

1. Piece a half-square triangle to a quarter-square triangle, lining up the outer corners. Press as the arrows indicate.

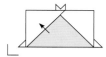

Line up outside corners.

2. Repeat Step 1 for the other side. Press.

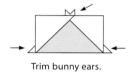

Repeat for other side.

3. Trim off the bunny ears.

Trim bunny ears.

4. Lay out 8 Flying Geese units as shown.

5. Sew the Flying Geese blocks together to form a large block. Piece and press as the arrows indicate. Repeat to form 4 large blocks.

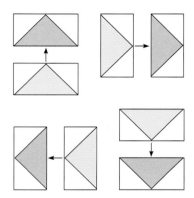

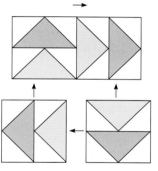

6. Sew the blocks into rows and press. Sew the rows together (page 15). Refer to page 15 for pressing.

Your quilt top should measure 24½″ × 24½″. If it does, use the instructions that follow to cut and attach the inner and outer border strips. If it doesn't, see pages 15–16 to measure and cut the correct border lengths for your quilt top.

(page 15). Refer to page 15 for pressing.

INNER BORDER

7. Cut 2 strips 1½″ × 24½″ for the top and bottom and 2 strips 1½″ × 26½″ for the sides.

8. Sew on the top and bottom inner border, then the sides. Refer to page 15 for pressing.

OUTER BORDER

9. Cut 2 strips 4½″ × 26½″ for the top and bottom and 2 strips 4½″ × 34½″ for the sides.

10. Sew on the top and bottom outer border, then the sides. Press.

Now it's time to consider the backing, quilting, and binding. See pages 16–21 for guidance. You will use this classic quilt block in many future quilts.

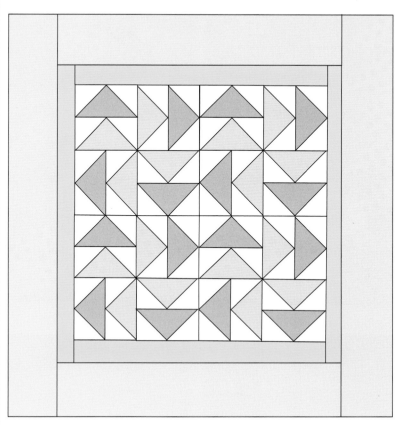

Flying Geese quilt

Wild Goose Run Quilt

Some of today's fabulous fabrics are too beautiful—or too much fun—to be cut into little pieces. This design provides the perfect showcase. Note the striped inner border . . . and keep your eyes peeled for polka dots, which add a wonderful sense of whimsy.

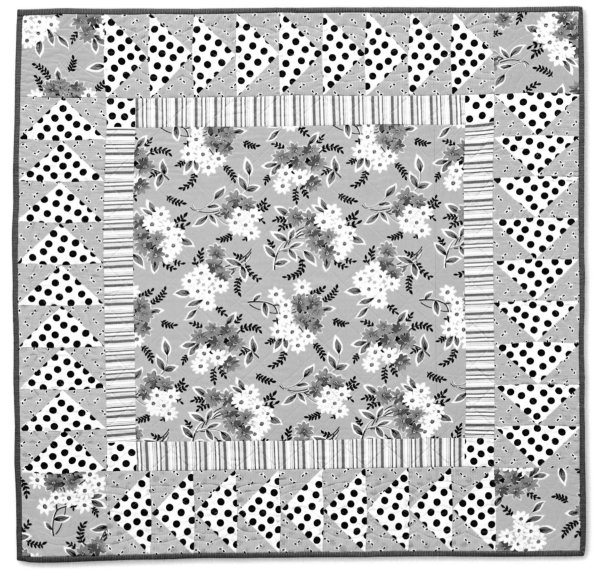

This quilt measures 39½″ × 39½″ and contains thirty-six 3″ × 6″ finished Flying Geese units. Pieced and machine quilted by Pam Vieira-McGinnis.

Fabric Requirements

Fabric requirements are based on 42″ fabric width.

- Focus fabric (A): ¾ yard for center panel and outer border corner squares

- Stripe (B): ⅜ yard for inner border

- Polka dot (C): ⅞ yard for inner border corner squares and geese

- Yellow print (D): ⅞ yard for geese background

- Binding: ⅜ yard

- Backing: 44″ × 44″

Please read The Basics (pages 11–21) before starting.

It is very important to always have the outside edge of the block on the straight of grain. This avoids unnecessary stretching. The sew-and-flip method of piecing the Flying Geese borders puts the straight of grain in just the right places. No thinking necessary.

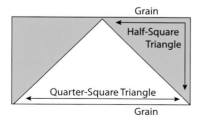

Grain for Flying Geese units

Flying Geese

Flying Geese unit

Cutting

Fabric A:

- Cut 1 square 23½″ × 23½″ for center panel.

- Cut 4 squares 6½″ × 6½″ for outer border corner squares.

Fabric B:

- Cut 4 strips 2½″ × 23½″ for inner border.

Fabric C:

- Cut 4 squares 2½″ × 2½″ for inner border corner squares.

- Cut 36 rectangles 3½″ × 6½″ for geese.

Fabric D:

- Cut 72 squares 3½″ × 3½″ for geese background.

Piecing and Pressing

1. Sew a 2½″ × 23½″ Fabric B strip to opposite sides of the 23½″ center square. Press as the arrows indicate.

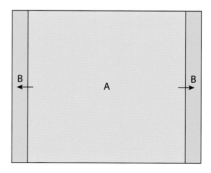

Sew B strips to A.

2. Sew a 2½″ Fabric C square to the ends of each remaining 2½″ Fabric B strip.

Sew C squares to B strips.

3. Sew to the top and bottom of the quilt top. Press as the arrows indicate.

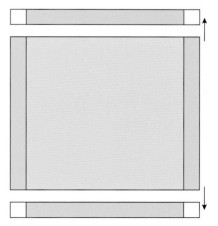

Add to the quilt top.

Border

4. Draw a line diagonally, corner to corner, on the wrong side of each 3½" Fabric D square.

5. Align a marked 3½" Fabric D square with one short edge of a 3½" × 6½" Fabric C rectangle, right sides together.

Place D on C.

6. Sew directly on the drawn line and trim, leaving a ¼" seam allowance. Press as the arrow indicates. Make 36.

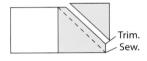

Sew D to C.

Press. Make 36.

7. Repeat Steps 5 and 6 to sew a 3½" Fabric D square to the opposite short edge of each unit from Step 6. Press as the arrow indicates.

Sew and press. Make 36.

8. Arrange 9 units. Sew the units together. Press as the arrows indicate. Refer to page 15 for pressing.

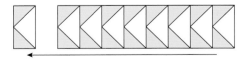

Sew and press. Make 4.

9. Sew a 6½" Fabric A square to each end of a border unit from Step 8. Make 2.

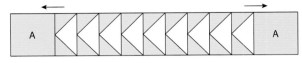

Sew A to a border unit. Make 2.

10. Sew a border unit from Step 8 to opposite sides of the quilt. Press as the arrows indicate. Sew a border unit from Step 9 to the top and bottom of the quilt top. Press as the arrows indicate.

Now it's time to consider the backing, quilting, and binding. See pages 16–21 for guidance. You will use this classic quilt block in many future quilts.

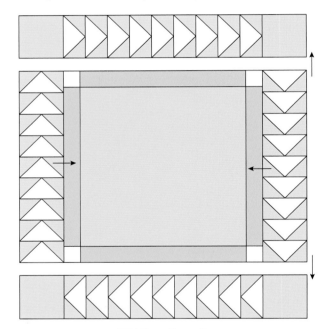

Wild Goose Run quilt

Sampler Quilt

Many of you will use this sampler as your first project from this book. Choose a focus print that speaks to you, and then purchase additional fabrics in colors to match. Have fun making the blocks, occasionally switching the value placement (e.g., substituting a dark background for a light). With a sampler quilt, each new block is an adventure!

This quilt measures 40½″ × 40½″ and contains twenty-five 6″ blocks. Pieced and machine quilted by Pam Vieira-McGinnis

Fabric Requirements

Fabric requirements are based on 42″ fabric width.

- Focus fabric: 1 yard for outer border

- Red (3–4 different fabrics*): ⅓ yard each

- Green (3–4 different fabrics*): ⅓ yard each

- Light neutrals (2 different fabrics*): ⅓ yard each

- Medium to dark neutrals (2 different fabrics*): ⅓ yard each

* Be sure to have a complete range of value from light to dark

- Plaid: ¼ yard for inner border

- Binding: ⅜ yard

- Backing: 1¼ yards

Samplers are a wonderful way to expose yourself to many different techniques without committing to an entire project of one repeated block. Your lesson plan is simply to make blocks from each wallhanging in this book. Each block teaches a different technique. You can make as many of each block as you want. This sampler has 25 blocks and is the perfect size for a wallhanging. If you would like to make a larger quilt, simply purchase more fabric and make more blocks. It's as easy as that.

Please read The Basics (pages 11–21) before starting.

To complete the quilt pictured, you will need to make:

- 8 Rail Fence blocks, 6″ (finished)
- 5 Nine-Patch blocks, 6″ (finished)
- 2 Nine-Patch Variation blocks, 6″ (finished)
- 3 Log Cabin blocks, 6″ (finished)
- 3 Friendship Star blocks, 6″ (finished)
- 3 Flying Geese blocks, 6″ (finished)
- 1 Square Dance block, 6″ (finished)

Cutting and Piecing

RAIL FENCE BLOCKS
Refer to page 23 for guidance.

1. Cut 1 strip 2½″ × 42″ from each of the 3 different green fabrics.

2. Cut 3 rectangles 2½″ × 6½″ from each strip in Step 1. Set the leftover strips aside to use later.

3. Piece and press. Make 3.

4. Repeat Steps 1–3 with the 3 neutral fabrics. Make 3.

5. Repeat Steps 1–3 with the 3 red fabrics although you will only need to cut 2 rectangles from each strip. Make 2.

NINE-PATCH BLOCKS
Refer to page 25 for guidance.

Notice that I have switched the placement of some of the light and dark squares.

1. Cut 5 red squares 2½″ × 2½″.

2. Cut 4 light neutral squares 2½″ × 2½″.

3. Piece and press.

4. Repeat steps 1–3 with additional red/light neutral fabrics. Make 3. Vary the placement of the colors as shown.

5. Repeat Steps 1–3 with the light and dark green fabrics. Make 1.

NINE-PATCH VARIATION BLOCKS
Refer to pages 25–26 for guidance.

1. Cut 1 strip 1½″ × 42″ from a light neutral fabric and 1 strip 1½″ × 42″ from a dark neutral fabric.

2. Cut 8 dark neutral squares 1½″ × 1½″.

3. Cut 8 light neutral squares 1½″ × 1½″.

4. Cut 1 dark neutral square 2½″ × 2½″.

5. Cut 4 light neutral squares 2½″ × 2½″.

6. Piece and press. Make 1.

7. Repeat Steps 1–5 with the light and dark green fabrics. Make 1.

LOG CABIN BLOCKS
Refer to page 30 for guidance.

1. Cut 3 red squares 1½″ × 1½″ for the chimneys.

2. Cut 1½″ × 42″ strips from a variety of light and dark fabrics for the logs. You can also use leftovers.

3. Piece and press. Make 3.

SQUARE DANCE BLOCKS
Refer to page 28 for guidance.

1. Cut a 3½″ × 3½″ light neutral square.

2. Cut 2 matching red rectangles 2″ × 6½″ and 2 rectangles 2″ × 3½″.

3. Piece and press. Make 1.

FRIENDSHIP STAR BLOCKS

Refer to page 33 for guidance.

1. Cut 1 light neutral square 2½″ × 2½″ for the star center.

2. Cut 2 light neutral squares 2⅞″ × 2⅞″, then cut them in half diagonally from corner to corner for the star points.

3. Cut 4 red squares 2½″ × 2½″ for the background.

4. Cut 2 red squares 2⅞″ × 2⅞″, then cut them in half diagonally from corner to corner for the background.

5. Piece and press. Make 1.

6. Repeat Steps 1–5 with the light neutral and dark green and then with 2 neutrals. Make 1 of each.

FLYING GEESE BLOCKS

Refer to pages 37 and 40 for guidance.

1. Cut 1 light neutral square 7¼″ × 7¼″, then cut in half diagonally twice for the large triangle (you will use one and have 3 extra). Repeat using a second light neutral fabric.

2. Cut 1 dark neutral square 3⅞″ × 3⅞″, then cut in half diagonally from corner to corner for the small triangles. Repeat using a red fabric.

3. Piece and press. Make 1.

4. Repeat Steps 1–3 with the 4 dark fabrics for the large triangles and 4 light fabrics for the small triangles. Make 2 blocks.

Quilt Top Construction

1. Arrange the blocks.

2. Sew the blocks into rows and press. Sew the rows together (page 15). Press.

Your quilt top should measure 30½″ × 30½″. If it does, use the instructions that follow to cut and attach the inner and outer border strips. If it doesn't, see pages 15–16 to measure and cut the correct border lengths for your quilt top.

INNER BORDER

3. Cut 2 strips 1½″ × 30½″ for the sides and 2 strips 1½″ × 32½″ for the sides.

4. Sew on the inner border (first the shorter top and bottom strips, then the longer side strips). Press.

OUTER BORDER

5. Cut 2 strips 4½″ × 32½″ for the top and bottom and 2 strips 4½″ × 40½″ for the sides.

6. Sew on the outer border (first the shorter top and bottom strips, then the longer side strips). Press.

See pages 16–21 for guidance to finish your quilt.

Samplers have been around since almost the beginning of quiltmaking time. I never tire of them, and to this day, I still enjoy making them. Each has its own creative process and personality.

Sampler quilt

Regarding Borders:

The outer borders on these quilts are made using beautiful print (focus) fabrics. The yardage requirements for the outer borders have taken into consideration that each outer border strip will be cut in one continuous piece (cut lengthwise, parallel to the selvages), rather than multiple strips (cut crosswise, selvage to selvage) that would include unsightly seams. These focus fabrics are beautiful, so the leftovers will be a wonderful addition to your fabric collection.

The charts on the following pages will give you the yardage requirements and cutting instructions for twin, double/queen, and king comforter-style quilts. The widths of the borders are just suggestions; trust your eye and your quilt size requirements to determine the border widths that work for your quilt.

NINE-PATCH VARIATION QUILT

Please use the charts, along with the project instructions on pages 24–26, to make a twin, full/queen, or king quilt. Blocks are 6″ × 6″ finished.

Twin: 66½″ × 90½″; 11 × 15 blocks

Full/Queen: 90½″ × 90½″; 15 × 15 blocks

King: 102½″ × 90½″; 17 × 15 blocks

Materials

FABRIC	TWIN	FULL/QUEEN	KING
Black	1⅝ yards	2⅛ yards	2⅜ yards
Black-and-white print	1¾ yards	2⅛ yards	2⅜ yards
White	4⅞ yards	6⅛ yards	6⅞ yards
Binding	⅝ yard	¾ yard	¾ yard
Backing	5¾ yards	8½ yards	8½ yards
Batting	74″ × 98″	98″ × 98″	110″ × 98″

Cutting

FABRIC	TWIN Number of Strips	FULL/QUEEN Number of Strips	KING Number of Strips
Black	1½″ wide: 24 2½″ wide: 6	1½″ wide: 33 2½″ wide: 8	1½″ wide: 37 2½″ wide: 9
Black-and-white print	2½″ wide: 23	2½″ wide: 28	2½″ wide: 32
White	1½″ wide: 24 2½″ wide: 51	1½″ wide: 33 2½″ wide: 66	1½″ wide: 37 2½″ wide: 72
Binding	9	10	10

Number of Elements

	TWIN	FULL/QUEEN	KING
# 9-PATCH BLOCKS	82	112	127
ELEMENTS	Number of Elements	Number of Elements	Number of Elements
Set A	11	14	16
Segment A	164	224	254
Set B	6	7	8
Segment B	82	112	127
# Double 9-Patch Variation blocks	83	113	128
ELEMENTS	Number of Elements	Number of Elements	Number of Elements
Set C	24	33	37
Segment C	664	904	1024
4-Patch Blocks	332	452	512
White – 2½″ squares combined with 4-Patch blocks	Use 11- 2½″strips subcut into 166 squares	Use 15- 2½″ strips subcut into 226 squares	Use 16- 2½″ strips subcut into 256 squares
Set D	6	8	9
Segment D	83	113	128

RAIL FENCE QUILT

Please use the charts, along with the project instructions on pages 22–23, to make a twin, full/queen, or king quilt. Blocks are 6˝ × 6˝ finished.

Twin: 68½˝ × 86½˝; 10 × 13 blocks, 1½˝ (cut size) inner border, 3½˝ (cut size) outer border

Full/Queen: 88½˝ × 94½˝; 12 × 13 blocks, 2½˝ (cut size) inner border, 6½˝ (cut size) outer border

King: 106½˝ × 94½˝; 15 × 13 blocks, 2½˝ (cut size) inner border, 6½˝ (cut size) outer border

Materials

FABRIC	TWIN	FULL/QUEEN	KING
Focus fabric	2⅜ yards	2⅝ yards	2¾ yards
Pink 3 different fabrics	⅝ yard of each	¾ yard of each	⅞ yard of each
Green 3 different fabrics	¾ yard of each	¾ yard of each	⅞ yard of each
Lavender 3 different fabrics	¾ yard of each	⅞ yard of each	1 yard of each
Print	⅜ yard	⅔ yard	¾ yard
Binding	⅝ yard	¾ yard	⅞ yard
Backing	5½ yards	8¼ yards	8¾ yards
Batting	76˝ × 94˝	96˝ × 102˝	114˝ × 102˝

Cutting

FABRIC	TWIN Number of Strips	FULL/QUEEN Number of Strips	KING Number of Strips
Focus fabric	Cut 4 strips from lengthwise grain (parallel to selvage).		
Pink	39 blocks 7 strips of each fabric	48 blocks 8 strips of each fabric	61 blocks 11 strips of each fabric
Green	44 blocks 8 strips of each fabric	51 blocks 9 strips of each fabric	64 blocks 11 strips of each fabric
Lavender	47 blocks 8 strips of each fabric	57 blocks 10 strips of each fabric	70 blocks 12 strips of each fabric
Print*	7	8	9
Binding	8	10	11

*Cut inner border strips the width shown in the sizing information above. Join inner border strips at their ends to make 1 long strip. Measure quilt top and cut borders to correct length as described on pages 15–16.

SQUARE DANCE QUILT

Please use the charts, along with the project instructions on pages 27–28, to make a twin, full/queen, or king quilt. Blocks are 6˝ × 6˝ finished.

Twin: 70½˝ × 88½˝; 10 × 13 blocks, 2˝ (cut size) inner border, 4˝ (cut size) outer border

Full/Queen: 87½˝ × 93½˝; 12 × 13 blocks, 2˝ (cut size) inner border, 6½˝ (cut size) outer border

King: 105½˝ × 93½˝; 15 × 13 blocks, 2˝ (cut size) inner border, 6½˝ (cut size) outer border

Materials

FABRIC	TWIN	FULL/QUEEN	KING
Assorted coordinating pink, green, purple, yellow, and tan batiks (A)	1⅝ yards total	1¾ yards total	2¼ yards total
Assorted coordinating pink, green, purple, yellow, and tan batiks (B)	4 yards total	5 yards total	6¼ yards total
Pink (C)	½ yard	½ yard	⅝ yard
Multicolored print (D)	2⅜ yards	2⅝ yards	2¾ yards
Binding	⅝ yard	¾ yard	¾ yard
Backing	5⅝ yards	8¼ yards	8¾ yards
Batting	78˝ × 96˝	95˝ × 101˝	113˝ × 101˝

Cutting

FABRIC	TWIN Number of Pieces	FULL/QUEEN Number of Pieces	KING Number of Pieces
Assorted coordinating pink, green, purple, yellow, and tan batiks (A)	130 total squares 3½˝ × 3½˝	156 total squares 3½˝ × 3½˝	195 total squares 3½˝ × 3½˝
Assorted coordinating pink, green, purple, yellow, and tan batiks (B)	260 – 2˝ × 3½˝ 260 – 2˝ × 6½˝	312 – 2˝ × 3½˝ 312 – 2˝ × 6½˝	390 – 2˝ × 3½˝ 390 – 2˝ × 6½˝
Pink* (C)	7 strips	8 strips	9 strips
Multicolored print (D)	Cut 4 strips from lengthwise grain (parallel to selvage).		
Binding	9	10	11

*Cut inner border strips the width shown in the sizing information above. Join inner border strips at their ends to make 1 long strip. Measure quilt top and cut borders to correct length as described on pages 15–16.

FRIENDSHIP STAR QUILT

Please use the charts, along with the project instructions on pages 32–34 to make a twin, full/queen, or king size quilt. Blocks are 6″ × 6″ finished.

Twin: 68½″ × 86½″; 10 × 13 blocks, 1½″ (cut size) inner border, 3½″ (cut size) outer border

Full/Queen: 88½″ × 94½″; 12 × 13 blocks, 2½″ (cut size) inner border, 6½″ (cut size) outer border

King: 106½″ × 94½″; 15 × 13 blocks, 2½″ (cut size) inner border, 6½″ (cut size) outer border

Materials

FABRIC	TWIN	FULL/ QUEEN	KING
Focus fabric	2⅜ yards	2⅝ yards	2¾ yards
Orange prints— 2 different fabrics	1⅜ yards of each	1½ yards of each	1⅞ yards of each
Green prints— 9 different fabrics	⅔ yard of each	¾ yard of each	1 yard of each
Print #2	⅜ yard	⅝ yard	¾ yard
Binding	⅝ yard	¾ yard	¾ yard
Backing	5½ yards	8¼ yards	8¾ yards
Batting	76″ × 94″	96″ × 102″	114″ × 102″

Note: Horizontal sashing (print #1) shown in the wallhanging quilt is not included in larger size quilts.

Cutting

FABRIC	TWIN Number of Pieces	FULL/QUEEN Number of Pieces	KING Number of Pieces
Focus fabric	Cut 4 strips from the lengthwise grain (parallel to selvage).		
Orange prints**	5 strips 2½″ wide from each fabric; subcut into 65 squares 2½″ × 2½″ (130 total); 10 strips 2⅞″ wide from each fabric; subcut into 130 squares, 2⅞″ × 2⅞″ (260 total); cut diagonally into 260 triangles (520 total)	5 strips 2½″ wide from each fabric; subcut into 78 squares 2½″ × 2½″ (156 total); 12 strips 2⅞″ wide from each fabric; subcut into 156 squares, 2⅞″ × 2⅞″ (312 total); cut diagonally into 312 triangles (624 total)	7 strips 2½″ wide from each fabric; subcut into 98 squares 2½″ × 2½″ (196 total); 14 strips 2⅞″ wide from each fabric; subcut into 195 squares, 2⅞″ × 2⅞″ (390 total); cut diagonally into 390 triangles (780 total)
Green prints**	4 strips 2½″ wide from each fabric; subcut into 60 squares 2½″ × 2½″ (540 total); 3 strips 2⅞″ wide from each fabric; subcut into 30 squares, 2⅞″ × 2⅞″ (270 total); cut diagonally into 60 triangles (540 total)	5 strips 2½″ wide from each fabric; subcut into 72 squares 2½″ × 2½″ (648 total); 3 strips 2⅞″ wide from each fabric; subcut into 36 squares, 2⅞″ × 2⅞″ (324 total); cut diagonally into 72 triangles (648 total)	6 strips 2½″ wide from each fabric; subcut into 88 squares 2½″ × 2½″ (792 total); 4 strips 2⅞″ wide from each fabric; subcut into 44 squares, 2⅞″ × 2⅞″ (396 total); cut diagonally into 88 triangles (792 total)
Print #2*	7 strips	8 strips	9 strips
Binding	8 strips	10 strips	11 strips

*Cut inner border strips the width shown in the sizing information above. Join inner border strips at their ends to make 1 long strip. Measure quilt top and cut borders to correct length as described on pages 15–16.
**You will have extra squares and triangles.

FLYING GEESE QUILT

Please use the charts, along with the project instructions on pages 35–37, to make a twin, full/queen, or king size quilt. Blocks are 6˝ × 6˝ finished.

Twin: 76½˝ × 88½˝; 10 × 12 blocks, 2½˝ (cut size) inner border, 6½˝ (cut size) outer border

Full/Queen: 88½˝ × 100½˝; 12 × 14 blocks, 2½˝ (cut size) inner border, 6½˝ (cut size) outer border

King: 100½˝ × 100½˝; 14 × 14 blocks, 2½˝ (cut size) inner border, 6½˝ (cut size) outer border

Materials

FABRIC	TWIN	FULL/QUEEN	KING
Focus fabric	2¼ yards	2⅝ yards	3 yards
Green— 2 different fabrics	⅞ yard of each	1¼ yards of each	1¼ yards of each
Blue— 2 different fabrics	⅞ yard of each	1¼ yards of each	1¼ yards of each
White	2⅞ yards	4 yards	4⅝ yards
Print	⅝ yard	⅝ yard	¾ yard
Binding	⅝ yard	¾ yard	¾ yard
Backing	5⅝ yards	8¼ yards	9¼ yards
Batting	84˝ × 96˝	96˝ × 108˝	108˝ × 108˝

Cutting

	TWIN	FULL/QUEEN	KING
FABRIC	Number of Pieces	Number of Pieces	Number of Pieces
Focus fabric	Cut 4 strips from the lengthwise grain (parallel to selvage).		
Green	15 squares from each fabric	21 squares from each fabric	25 squares from each fabric**
Blue	15 squares from each fabric	21 squares from each fabric	25 squares from each fabric**
White	240 squares	336 squares	392 squares
Print*	7 strips	8 strips	9 strips
Binding	9	10	11

*Cut inner border strips the width shown in the sizing information above. Join inner border strips at their ends to make 1 long strip. Measure quilt top and cut borders to correct length as described on pages 15–16.
**You will have extra triangles.

LOG CABIN VARIATION QUILT

Please use the charts, along with the project instructions on pages 29–31 to make a twin, full/queen, or king size quilt. Blocks are 6˝ × 6˝ finished.

Twin: 68½˝ × 92½˝; 10 × 14 blocks, 1½˝ (cut size) inner border, 3½˝ (cut size) outer border

Full/Queen: 88½˝ × 94½˝; 12 × 13 blocks, 2½˝ (cut size) inner border, 6½˝ (cut size) outer border

King: 106½˝ × 94½˝; 15 × 13 blocks, 2½˝ (cut size) inner border, 6½˝ (cut size) outer border

Materials

FABRIC	TWIN	FULL/QUEEN	KING
Print #1 (focus fabric)	2½ yards	2⅝ yards	2¾ yards
Red	¼ yard	⅓ yard	⅓ yard
Darks— 6 different fabrics	¾ yard of each	⅞ yard of each	1⅛ yard of each
Lights— 4 different fabrics	⅔ yard of each	¾ yard of each	⅞ yard of each
Print #2	⅜ yard	⅝ yard	¾ yard
Binding	⅝ yard	¾ yard	¾ yard
Backing	5⅞ yards	8¼ yards	9 yards
Batting	76˝ × 100˝	96˝ × 102˝	114˝ × 102˝

Cutting

	TWIN	FULL/QUEEN	KING
FABRIC	Number of Strips	Number of Strips	Number of Strips
Print #1	Cut 4 strips from the lengthwise grain (parallel to selvage).		
Red	5	6	7
Darks	17 of each fabric	20 of each fabric	24 of each fabric
Lights	15 of each fabric	16 of each fabric	20 of each fabric
Print #2*	7	8	9
Binding	9	10	11

*Cut inner border strips the width shown in the sizing information above. Join inner border strips at their ends to make 1 long strip. Measure quilt top and cut borders to correct length as described on pages 15–16.

About the Author

Alex Anderson's love affair with quiltmaking began in 1978, when she completed her grandmother's Flower Garden quilt as part of her work toward a degree in art at San Francisco State University. Over the years, her central focus has rested on understanding fabric relationships and on an intense appreciation of traditional quilting surface design and star quilts.

Alex currently co-hosts The Quilt Show (www.thequiltshow.com) with Ricky Tims. Her quilts have been shown in magazines, including several articles specifically about her works. Visit her website at alexandersonquilts.com.

Alex lives in California, with her husband.

Also by Alex Anderson:

Great Titles *from* C&T PUBLISHING

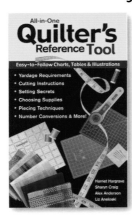   

Available at your local retailer or **www.ctpub.com** *or* **800.284.1114**

For a list of other fine books from C&T Publishing, ask for a free catalog:

C&T PUBLISHING, INC.

P.O. Box 1456
Lafayette, CA 94549
(800) 284-1114

Email: ctinfo@ctpub.com
Website: www.ctpub.com

C&T Publishing's professional photography services are now available to the public. Visit us at www.ctmediaservices.com.

For quilting supplies:

COTTON PATCH

1025 Brown Ave.
Lafayette, CA 94549
Store: (925) 284-1177
Mail order: (925) 283-7883

Email: CottonPa@aol.com
Website: www.quiltusa.com

Note: Fabrics used in the quilts shown may not be currently available, as fabric manufacturers keep most fabrics in print for only a short time.